This Book Belongs To:

_____

_____

_____

Copyright © Teresa Rother
All rights reserved. No part of this publication may be reproduced, distributed, or transmitted in any form or by any means, including photocopy, recording, or other electronic or mechanical methods.

DEDICATION

This Book Report Log is dedicated to all the kids who need help with structuring and organizing book report assignments and want to comprehend what they are reading by recording the information.

You are my inspiration for producing this book and I'm honored to be a part of helping you manage and retain important information regarding your reading assignments and book reports.

HOW TO USE THIS BOOK

This Book Report Log Book will help you record, collect, and organize your information in an easy to use format.

Here are examples of information for you to fill in and write the details for your assignments.

Fill in the following information:

1. Table of Contents - page numbers 1-87, place to record book title, start date, end date, and the total number of pages

2. Book Report - Record Title, Author, Main Characters, Story Setting, Story Summary, Main Events, Story Conclusion, Write One Fact and One Opinion, About The Story

TABLE OF CONTENTS

PAGE #	TITLE	START DATE	END DATE	PAGE TOTAL
1				
2				
3				
4				
5				
6				
7				
8				
9				
10				
11				
12				
13				
14				
15				
16				
17				
18				
19				
20				
21				
22				
23				
24				
25				
26				
27				
28				
29				

TABLE OF CONTENTS

PAGE #	TITLE	START DATE	END DATE	PAGE TOTAL
30				
31				
32				
33				
34				
35				
36				
37				
38				
39				
40				
41				
42				
43				
44				
45				
46				
47				
48				
49				
50				
51				
52				
53				
54				
55				
56				
57				
58				

TABLE OF CONTENTS

PAGE #	TITLE	START DATE	END DATE	PAGE TOTAL
59				
60				
61				
62				
63				
64				
65				
66				
67				
68				
69				
70				
71				
72				
73				
74				
75				
76				
77				
78				
79				
80				
81				
82				
83				
84				
85				
86				
87				

BOOK REPORT

TITLE

AUTHOR

MAIN CHARACTERS

STORY SETTING

STORY SUMMARY

MAIN EVENTS

STORY CONCLUSION

WRITE ONE FACT AND ONE OPINION ABOUT THIS STORY

FACT:

OPINION:

BOOK REPORT

TITLE	
AUTHOR	

MAIN CHARACTERS	STORY SETTING

STORY SUMMARY

MAIN EVENTS

STORY CONCLUSION

WRITE ONE FACT AND ONE OPINION ABOUT THIS STORY

FACT:

OPINION:

BOOK REPORT

TITLE	
AUTHOR	

MAIN CHARACTERS	STORY SETTING

STORY SUMMARY

MAIN EVENTS

STORY CONCLUSION

WRITE ONE FACT AND ONE OPINION ABOUT THIS STORY

FACT:

OPINION:

BOOK REPORT

TITLE	
AUTHOR	

MAIN CHARACTERS	STORY SETTING

STORY SUMMARY

MAIN EVENTS

STORY CONCLUSION

WRITE ONE FACT AND ONE OPINION ABOUT THIS STORY

FACT:

OPINION:

BOOK REPORT

TITLE	
AUTHOR	

MAIN CHARACTERS	STORY SETTING

STORY SUMMARY

MAIN EVENTS

STORY CONCLUSION

WRITE ONE FACT AND ONE OPINION ABOUT THIS STORY

FACT:

OPINION:

BOOK REPORT

TITLE	
AUTHOR	

MAIN CHARACTERS	STORY SETTING

STORY SUMMARY

MAIN EVENTS

STORY CONCLUSION

WRITE ONE FACT AND ONE OPINION ABOUT THIS STORY

FACT:

OPINION:

BOOK REPORT

TITLE	
AUTHOR	

MAIN CHARACTERS	STORY SETTING

STORY SUMMARY

MAIN EVENTS

STORY CONCLUSION

WRITE ONE FACT AND ONE OPINION ABOUT THIS STORY

FACT:

OPINION:

BOOK REPORT

TITLE	
AUTHOR	

MAIN CHARACTERS	STORY SETTING

STORY SUMMARY

MAIN EVENTS

STORY CONCLUSION

WRITE ONE FACT AND ONE OPINION ABOUT THIS STORY

FACT:

OPINION:

BOOK REPORT

TITLE	
AUTHOR	

MAIN CHARACTERS	STORY SETTING

STORY SUMMARY

MAIN EVENTS

STORY CONCLUSION

WRITE ONE FACT AND ONE OPINION ABOUT THIS STORY

FACT:

OPINION:

BOOK REPORT

TITLE	
AUTHOR	

MAIN CHARACTERS	STORY SETTING

STORY SUMMARY

MAIN EVENTS

STORY CONCLUSION

WRITE ONE FACT AND ONE OPINION ABOUT THIS STORY

FACT:

OPINION:

BOOK REPORT

TITLE	
AUTHOR	

MAIN CHARACTERS	STORY SETTING

STORY SUMMARY

MAIN EVENTS

STORY CONCLUSION

WRITE ONE FACT AND ONE OPINION ABOUT THIS STORY

FACT:

OPINION:

BOOK REPORT

TITLE	
AUTHOR	

MAIN CHARACTERS	STORY SETTING

STORY SUMMARY

MAIN EVENTS

STORY CONCLUSION

WRITE ONE FACT AND ONE OPINION ABOUT THIS STORY

FACT:

OPINION:

BOOK REPORT

TITLE	
AUTHOR	

MAIN CHARACTERS	STORY SETTING

STORY SUMMARY

MAIN EVENTS

STORY CONCLUSION

WRITE ONE FACT AND ONE OPINION ABOUT THIS STORY

FACT:

OPINION:

13

BOOK REPORT

TITLE	
AUTHOR	

MAIN CHARACTERS	STORY SETTING

STORY SUMMARY

MAIN EVENTS

STORY CONCLUSION

WRITE ONE FACT AND ONE OPINION ABOUT THIS STORY

FACT:

OPINION:

BOOK REPORT

TITLE	
AUTHOR	

MAIN CHARACTERS	STORY SETTING

STORY SUMMARY

MAIN EVENTS

STORY CONCLUSION

WRITE ONE FACT AND ONE OPINION ABOUT THIS STORY

FACT:

OPINION:

BOOK REPORT

TITLE	
AUTHOR	

MAIN CHARACTERS	STORY SETTING

STORY SUMMARY

MAIN EVENTS

STORY CONCLUSION

WRITE ONE FACT AND ONE OPINION ABOUT THIS STORY

FACT:

OPINION:

BOOK REPORT

TITLE	
AUTHOR	

MAIN CHARACTERS	STORY SETTING

STORY SUMMARY

MAIN EVENTS

STORY CONCLUSION

WRITE ONE FACT AND ONE OPINION ABOUT THIS STORY

FACT:

OPINION:

BOOK REPORT

TITLE	
AUTHOR	

MAIN CHARACTERS	STORY SETTING

STORY SUMMARY

MAIN EVENTS

STORY CONCLUSION

WRITE ONE FACT AND ONE OPINION ABOUT THIS STORY

FACT:

OPINION:

BOOK REPORT

TITLE	
AUTHOR	

MAIN CHARACTERS	STORY SETTING

STORY SUMMARY

MAIN EVENTS

STORY CONCLUSION

WRITE ONE FACT AND ONE OPINION ABOUT THIS STORY

FACT:

OPINION:

BOOK REPORT

TITLE	
AUTHOR	

MAIN CHARACTERS	STORY SETTING

STORY SUMMARY

MAIN EVENTS

STORY CONCLUSION

WRITE ONE FACT AND ONE OPINION ABOUT THIS STORY

FACT:

OPINION:

BOOK REPORT

TITLE	

AUTHOR	

MAIN CHARACTERS	STORY SETTING

STORY SUMMARY

MAIN EVENTS

STORY CONCLUSION

WRITE ONE FACT AND ONE OPINION ABOUT THIS STORY

FACT:

OPINION:

BOOK REPORT

TITLE	
AUTHOR	

MAIN CHARACTERS	STORY SETTING

STORY SUMMARY

MAIN EVENTS

STORY CONCLUSION

WRITE ONE FACT AND ONE OPINION ABOUT THIS STORY

FACT:

OPINION:

BOOK REPORT

TITLE	
AUTHOR	

MAIN CHARACTERS	STORY SETTING

STORY SUMMARY

MAIN EVENTS

STORY CONCLUSION

WRITE ONE FACT AND ONE OPINION ABOUT THIS STORY

FACT:

OPINION:

BOOK REPORT

TITLE	
AUTHOR	

MAIN CHARACTERS	STORY SETTING

STORY SUMMARY

MAIN EVENTS

STORY CONCLUSION

WRITE ONE FACT AND ONE OPINION ABOUT THIS STORY

FACT:

OPINION:

BOOK REPORT

TITLE	
AUTHOR	

MAIN CHARACTERS	STORY SETTING

STORY SUMMARY

MAIN EVENTS

STORY CONCLUSION

WRITE ONE FACT AND ONE OPINION ABOUT THIS STORY

FACT:

OPINION:

BOOK REPORT

TITLE	
AUTHOR	

MAIN CHARACTERS	STORY SETTING

STORY SUMMARY

MAIN EVENTS

STORY CONCLUSION

WRITE ONE FACT AND ONE OPINION ABOUT THIS STORY

FACT:

OPINION:

BOOK REPORT

TITLE	
AUTHOR	

MAIN CHARACTERS	STORY SETTING

STORY SUMMARY

MAIN EVENTS

STORY CONCLUSION

WRITE ONE FACT AND ONE OPINION ABOUT THIS STORY

FACT:

OPINION:

BOOK REPORT

TITLE	
AUTHOR	

MAIN CHARACTERS	STORY SETTING

STORY SUMMARY

MAIN EVENTS

STORY CONCLUSION

WRITE ONE FACT AND ONE OPINION ABOUT THIS STORY

FACT:

OPINION:

BOOK REPORT

TITLE	
AUTHOR	

MAIN CHARACTERS	STORY SETTING

STORY SUMMARY

MAIN EVENTS

STORY CONCLUSION

WRITE ONE FACT AND ONE OPINION ABOUT THIS STORY

FACT:

OPINION:

BOOK REPORT

TITLE	
AUTHOR	

MAIN CHARACTERS	STORY SETTING

STORY SUMMARY

MAIN EVENTS

STORY CONCLUSION

WRITE ONE FACT AND ONE OPINION ABOUT THIS STORY

FACT:

OPINION:

BOOK REPORT

TITLE	
AUTHOR	

MAIN CHARACTERS	STORY SETTING

STORY SUMMARY

MAIN EVENTS

STORY CONCLUSION

WRITE ONE FACT AND ONE OPINION ABOUT THIS STORY

FACT:

OPINION:

BOOK REPORT

TITLE	
AUTHOR	

MAIN CHARACTERS	STORY SETTING

STORY SUMMARY

MAIN EVENTS

STORY CONCLUSION

WRITE ONE FACT AND ONE OPINION ABOUT THIS STORY

FACT:

OPINION:

BOOK REPORT

TITLE	
AUTHOR	

MAIN CHARACTERS	STORY SETTING

STORY SUMMARY

MAIN EVENTS

STORY CONCLUSION

WRITE ONE FACT AND ONE OPINION ABOUT THIS STORY

FACT:

OPINION:

BOOK REPORT

TITLE	
AUTHOR	

MAIN CHARACTERS	STORY SETTING

STORY SUMMARY

MAIN EVENTS

STORY CONCLUSION

WRITE ONE FACT AND ONE OPINION ABOUT THIS STORY

FACT:

OPINION:

BOOK REPORT

TITLE	
AUTHOR	

MAIN CHARACTERS	STORY SETTING

STORY SUMMARY

MAIN EVENTS

STORY CONCLUSION

WRITE ONE FACT AND ONE OPINION ABOUT THIS STORY

FACT:

OPINION:

BOOK REPORT

TITLE	
AUTHOR	

MAIN CHARACTERS	STORY SETTING

STORY SUMMARY

MAIN EVENTS

STORY CONCLUSION

WRITE ONE FACT AND ONE OPINION ABOUT THIS STORY

FACT:

OPINION:

BOOK REPORT

TITLE	
AUTHOR	

MAIN CHARACTERS	STORY SETTING

STORY SUMMARY

MAIN EVENTS

STORY CONCLUSION

WRITE ONE FACT AND ONE OPINION ABOUT THIS STORY

FACT:

OPINION:

BOOK REPORT

TITLE	
AUTHOR	

MAIN CHARACTERS	STORY SETTING

STORY SUMMARY

MAIN EVENTS

STORY CONCLUSION

WRITE ONE FACT AND ONE OPINION ABOUT THIS STORY

FACT:

OPINION:

BOOK REPORT

TITLE	
AUTHOR	

MAIN CHARACTERS	STORY SETTING

STORY SUMMARY

MAIN EVENTS

STORY CONCLUSION

WRITE ONE FACT AND ONE OPINION ABOUT THIS STORY

FACT:

OPINION:

BOOK REPORT

TITLE	
AUTHOR	

MAIN CHARACTERS	STORY SETTING

STORY SUMMARY

MAIN EVENTS

STORY CONCLUSION

WRITE ONE FACT AND ONE OPINION ABOUT THIS STORY

FACT:

OPINION:

BOOK REPORT

TITLE	
AUTHOR	

MAIN CHARACTERS	STORY SETTING

STORY SUMMARY

MAIN EVENTS

STORY CONCLUSION

WRITE ONE FACT AND ONE OPINION ABOUT THIS STORY

FACT:

OPINION:

BOOK REPORT

TITLE	
AUTHOR	

MAIN CHARACTERS	STORY SETTING

STORY SUMMARY

MAIN EVENTS

STORY CONCLUSION

WRITE ONE FACT AND ONE OPINION ABOUT THIS STORY

FACT:

OPINION:

BOOK REPORT

TITLE	
AUTHOR	

MAIN CHARACTERS	STORY SETTING

STORY SUMMARY

MAIN EVENTS

STORY CONCLUSION

WRITE ONE FACT AND ONE OPINION ABOUT THIS STORY

FACT:

OPINION:

BOOK REPORT

TITLE	
AUTHOR	

MAIN CHARACTERS	STORY SETTING

STORY SUMMARY

MAIN EVENTS

STORY CONCLUSION

WRITE ONE FACT AND ONE OPINION ABOUT THIS STORY

FACT:

OPINION:

BOOK REPORT

TITLE	
AUTHOR	

MAIN CHARACTERS	STORY SETTING

STORY SUMMARY

MAIN EVENTS

STORY CONCLUSION

WRITE ONE FACT AND ONE OPINION ABOUT THIS STORY

FACT:

OPINION:

BOOK REPORT

TITLE	
AUTHOR	

MAIN CHARACTERS	STORY SETTING

STORY SUMMARY

MAIN EVENTS

STORY CONCLUSION

WRITE ONE FACT AND ONE OPINION ABOUT THIS STORY

FACT:

OPINION:

BOOK REPORT

TITLE	
AUTHOR	

MAIN CHARACTERS	STORY SETTING

STORY SUMMARY

MAIN EVENTS

STORY CONCLUSION

WRITE ONE FACT AND ONE OPINION ABOUT THIS STORY

FACT:

OPINION:

BOOK REPORT

TITLE	
AUTHOR	

MAIN CHARACTERS	STORY SETTING

STORY SUMMARY

MAIN EVENTS

STORY CONCLUSION

WRITE ONE FACT AND ONE OPINION ABOUT THIS STORY

FACT:

OPINION:

BOOK REPORT

TITLE	
AUTHOR	

MAIN CHARACTERS	STORY SETTING

STORY SUMMARY

MAIN EVENTS

STORY CONCLUSION

WRITE ONE FACT AND ONE OPINION ABOUT THIS STORY

FACT:

OPINION:

BOOK REPORT

TITLE	
AUTHOR	

MAIN CHARACTERS	STORY SETTING

STORY SUMMARY

MAIN EVENTS

STORY CONCLUSION

WRITE ONE FACT AND ONE OPINION ABOUT THIS STORY

FACT:

OPINION:

BOOK REPORT

TITLE	
AUTHOR	

MAIN CHARACTERS	STORY SETTING

STORY SUMMARY

MAIN EVENTS

STORY CONCLUSION

WRITE ONE FACT AND ONE OPINION ABOUT THIS STORY

FACT:

OPINION:

BOOK REPORT

TITLE	
AUTHOR	

MAIN CHARACTERS	STORY SETTING

STORY SUMMARY

MAIN EVENTS

STORY CONCLUSION

WRITE ONE FACT AND ONE OPINION ABOUT THIS STORY

FACT:

OPINION:

BOOK REPORT

TITLE	
AUTHOR	

MAIN CHARACTERS	STORY SETTING

STORY SUMMARY

MAIN EVENTS

STORY CONCLUSION

WRITE ONE FACT AND ONE OPINION ABOUT THIS STORY

FACT:

OPINION:

BOOK REPORT

TITLE	
AUTHOR	

MAIN CHARACTERS	STORY SETTING

STORY SUMMARY

MAIN EVENTS

STORY CONCLUSION

WRITE ONE FACT AND ONE OPINION ABOUT THIS STORY

FACT:

OPINION:

BOOK REPORT

TITLE	
AUTHOR	

MAIN CHARACTERS	STORY SETTING

STORY SUMMARY

MAIN EVENTS

STORY CONCLUSION

WRITE ONE FACT AND ONE OPINION ABOUT THIS STORY

FACT:

OPINION:

BOOK REPORT

TITLE	
AUTHOR	

MAIN CHARACTERS	STORY SETTING

STORY SUMMARY

MAIN EVENTS

STORY CONCLUSION

WRITE ONE FACT AND ONE OPINION ABOUT THIS STORY

FACT:

OPINION:

BOOK REPORT

TITLE	
AUTHOR	

MAIN CHARACTERS	STORY SETTING

STORY SUMMARY

MAIN EVENTS

STORY CONCLUSION

WRITE ONE FACT AND ONE OPINION ABOUT THIS STORY

FACT:

OPINION:

BOOK REPORT

TITLE	
AUTHOR	

MAIN CHARACTERS	STORY SETTING

STORY SUMMARY

MAIN EVENTS

STORY CONCLUSION

WRITE ONE FACT AND ONE OPINION ABOUT THIS STORY

FACT:

OPINION:

BOOK REPORT

TITLE	
AUTHOR	

MAIN CHARACTERS	STORY SETTING

STORY SUMMARY

MAIN EVENTS

STORY CONCLUSION

WRITE ONE FACT AND ONE OPINION ABOUT THIS STORY

FACT:

OPINION:

BOOK REPORT

TITLE	
AUTHOR	

MAIN CHARACTERS	STORY SETTING

STORY SUMMARY

MAIN EVENTS

STORY CONCLUSION

WRITE ONE FACT AND ONE OPINION ABOUT THIS STORY

FACT:

OPINION:

BOOK REPORT

TITLE	
AUTHOR	

MAIN CHARACTERS	STORY SETTING

STORY SUMMARY

MAIN EVENTS

STORY CONCLUSION

WRITE ONE FACT AND ONE OPINION ABOUT THIS STORY

FACT:

OPINION:

BOOK REPORT

TITLE	
AUTHOR	

MAIN CHARACTERS	STORY SETTING

STORY SUMMARY

MAIN EVENTS

STORY CONCLUSION

WRITE ONE FACT AND ONE OPINION ABOUT THIS STORY

FACT:

OPINION:

BOOK REPORT

TITLE	
AUTHOR	

MAIN CHARACTERS	STORY SETTING

STORY SUMMARY

MAIN EVENTS

STORY CONCLUSION

WRITE ONE FACT AND ONE OPINION ABOUT THIS STORY

FACT:

OPINION:

BOOK REPORT

TITLE	
AUTHOR	

MAIN CHARACTERS	STORY SETTING

STORY SUMMARY

MAIN EVENTS

STORY CONCLUSION

WRITE ONE FACT AND ONE OPINION ABOUT THIS STORY

FACT:

OPINION:

BOOK REPORT

TITLE	
AUTHOR	

MAIN CHARACTERS	STORY SETTING

STORY SUMMARY

MAIN EVENTS

STORY CONCLUSION

WRITE ONE FACT AND ONE OPINION ABOUT THIS STORY

FACT:

OPINION:

BOOK REPORT

TITLE	
AUTHOR	

MAIN CHARACTERS	STORY SETTING

STORY SUMMARY

MAIN EVENTS

STORY CONCLUSION

WRITE ONE FACT AND ONE OPINION ABOUT THIS STORY

FACT:

OPINION:

BOOK REPORT

TITLE	
AUTHOR	

MAIN CHARACTERS	STORY SETTING

STORY SUMMARY

MAIN EVENTS

STORY CONCLUSION

WRITE ONE FACT AND ONE OPINION ABOUT THIS STORY

FACT:

OPINION:

BOOK REPORT

TITLE	
AUTHOR	

MAIN CHARACTERS	STORY SETTING

STORY SUMMARY

MAIN EVENTS

STORY CONCLUSION

WRITE ONE FACT AND ONE OPINION ABOUT THIS STORY

FACT:

OPINION:

BOOK REPORT

TITLE	
AUTHOR	

MAIN CHARACTERS	STORY SETTING

STORY SUMMARY

MAIN EVENTS

STORY CONCLUSION

WRITE ONE FACT AND ONE OPINION ABOUT THIS STORY

FACT:

OPINION:

BOOK REPORT

TITLE	
AUTHOR	

MAIN CHARACTERS	STORY SETTING

STORY SUMMARY

MAIN EVENTS

STORY CONCLUSION

WRITE ONE FACT AND ONE OPINION ABOUT THIS STORY

FACT:

OPINION:

BOOK REPORT

TITLE	
AUTHOR	

MAIN CHARACTERS	STORY SETTING

STORY SUMMARY

MAIN EVENTS

STORY CONCLUSION

WRITE ONE FACT AND ONE OPINION ABOUT THIS STORY

FACT:

OPINION:

BOOK REPORT

TITLE	
AUTHOR	

MAIN CHARACTERS	STORY SETTING

STORY SUMMARY

MAIN EVENTS

STORY CONCLUSION

WRITE ONE FACT AND ONE OPINION ABOUT THIS STORY

FACT:

OPINION:

BOOK REPORT

TITLE	
AUTHOR	

MAIN CHARACTERS	STORY SETTING

STORY SUMMARY

MAIN EVENTS

STORY CONCLUSION

WRITE ONE FACT AND ONE OPINION ABOUT THIS STORY

FACT:

OPINION:

BOOK REPORT

TITLE	
AUTHOR	

MAIN CHARACTERS	STORY SETTING

STORY SUMMARY

MAIN EVENTS

STORY CONCLUSION

WRITE ONE FACT AND ONE OPINION ABOUT THIS STORY

FACT:

OPINION:

BOOK REPORT

TITLE	
AUTHOR	

MAIN CHARACTERS	STORY SETTING

STORY SUMMARY

MAIN EVENTS

STORY CONCLUSION

WRITE ONE FACT AND ONE OPINION ABOUT THIS STORY

FACT:

OPINION:

BOOK REPORT

TITLE	
AUTHOR	

MAIN CHARACTERS	STORY SETTING

STORY SUMMARY

MAIN EVENTS

STORY CONCLUSION

WRITE ONE FACT AND ONE OPINION ABOUT THIS STORY

FACT:

OPINION:

BOOK REPORT

TITLE	
AUTHOR	

MAIN CHARACTERS	STORY SETTING

STORY SUMMARY

MAIN EVENTS

STORY CONCLUSION

WRITE ONE FACT AND ONE OPINION ABOUT THIS STORY

FACT:

OPINION:

BOOK REPORT

TITLE	
AUTHOR	

MAIN CHARACTERS	STORY SETTING

STORY SUMMARY

MAIN EVENTS

STORY CONCLUSION

WRITE ONE FACT AND ONE OPINION ABOUT THIS STORY

FACT:

OPINION:

BOOK REPORT

TITLE	
AUTHOR	

MAIN CHARACTERS	STORY SETTING

STORY SUMMARY

MAIN EVENTS

STORY CONCLUSION

WRITE ONE FACT AND ONE OPINION ABOUT THIS STORY

FACT:

OPINION:

BOOK REPORT

TITLE	
AUTHOR	

MAIN CHARACTERS	STORY SETTING

STORY SUMMARY

MAIN EVENTS

STORY CONCLUSION

WRITE ONE FACT AND ONE OPINION ABOUT THIS STORY

FACT:

OPINION:

BOOK REPORT

TITLE	
AUTHOR	

MAIN CHARACTERS	STORY SETTING

STORY SUMMARY

MAIN EVENTS

STORY CONCLUSION

WRITE ONE FACT AND ONE OPINION ABOUT THIS STORY

FACT:

OPINION:

BOOK REPORT

TITLE	
AUTHOR	

MAIN CHARACTERS	STORY SETTING

STORY SUMMARY

MAIN EVENTS

STORY CONCLUSION

WRITE ONE FACT AND ONE OPINION ABOUT THIS STORY

FACT:

OPINION:

BOOK REPORT

TITLE	
AUTHOR	

MAIN CHARACTERS	STORY SETTING

STORY SUMMARY

MAIN EVENTS

STORY CONCLUSION

WRITE ONE FACT AND ONE OPINION ABOUT THIS STORY

FACT:

OPINION:

BOOK REPORT

TITLE

AUTHOR

MAIN CHARACTERS

STORY SETTING

STORY SUMMARY

MAIN EVENTS

STORY CONCLUSION

WRITE ONE FACT AND ONE OPINION ABOUT THIS STORY

FACT:

OPINION:

BOOK REPORT

TITLE	
AUTHOR	

MAIN CHARACTERS	STORY SETTING

STORY SUMMARY

MAIN EVENTS

STORY CONCLUSION

WRITE ONE FACT AND ONE OPINION ABOUT THIS STORY

FACT:

OPINION:

BOOK REPORT

TITLE	
AUTHOR	

MAIN CHARACTERS	STORY SETTING

STORY SUMMARY

MAIN EVENTS

STORY CONCLUSION

WRITE ONE FACT AND ONE OPINION ABOUT THIS STORY

FACT:

OPINION:

BOOK REPORT

TITLE	
AUTHOR	

MAIN CHARACTERS	STORY SETTING

STORY SUMMARY

MAIN EVENTS

STORY CONCLUSION

WRITE ONE FACT AND ONE OPINION ABOUT THIS STORY

FACT:

OPINION:

www.ingramcontent.com/pod-product-compliance
Lightning Source LLC
Chambersburg PA
CBHW081157070526
44583CB00021B/2879